THE AMAZING EXCHANGE

Experiencing the Reality of Righteousness
in Your Everyday Life

Mary Forsythe

The Amazing Exchange

For information contact:
Kingdom Living Ministries
PO Box 703685
Dallas, Texas 75370
www.kingdomliving.com

ISBN: 978-0-9725683-5-7

Cover design by Vision Communications

Printed in the United States of America
1 2 3 4 5 6 7   12 11 10 9 08 07

Contents

Introduction

There are certain truths that are critical for us to comprehend in this hour. I am not talking about merely having "head knowledge," but about having revelation, which we can only receive from the Holy Spirit. I sense that one area He is focusing on and releasing fresh revelation about in the lives of God's people right now is the area of identity. I believe you and I are living in a time when we *must* understand who we are in God. He is not merely interested in the things we are doing for Him because He knows that we need to have a strong foundation of who we are before we really enter into fruitful work for Him and fulfill our destinies. Proverbs 10:25 says, "When the whirlwind passes by, the wicked is no more, but the righteous has an everlasting foundation."

It is inevitable that "the whirlwinds" will hit every one of our lives, so the question is: Will we have a foundation strong enough to not merely withstand the winds, but to come through them with victory, strength, peace and joy?

I want to invite and encourage you today to step back from the pressures of your everyday life and take some time to read and pray your way through this book, allowing the Holy Spirit to increase your revelation of a critical and often misunderstood element of your identity as a believer—your righteousness in Christ. I believe this is a very important aspect of your foundation that needs to be built now in preparation for what is yet to come in your life. The Lord has a great future and a hope for you, but in His mercy He does withhold many things until we are mature enough and ready to handle them. We must be prepared for the blessings and the storms that will touch our lives in the days to come, and one important aspect of the preparation process is to seek the Lord *now* for greater revelation of your identity.

As you live in the ever-deepening revelation of the righteousness that sets you free, you will not only discover and enjoy greater confidence, inner strength, stability and intimacy with God than you have ever experienced before, but you will also be empowered to move forward in the awesome plans He has for you.

Chapter One

"Go Find Yourself!"

I had just finished ministering at a retreat and was gathering my belongings to leave when a young woman stopped me and asked me to pray for her. As we took our seats, her pain was obvious. Tears began streaming down her cheeks as she said, "Mary, I just don't know who I am." Obviously, she was going through a serious identity crisis. Even though she was a wife, a mother and a Bible study teacher, she was not sure who she *really* was. She could articulate clearly her roles and functions, but not her *identity*. Her "do" was evident, but her "who" was yet to be discovered.

I looked her in the eye and said, "You are the righteousness of God in Christ. You are totally accepted because you are a born-again believer." In response, she bowed her head and said, "I could *never* say that about myself. You don't know what I've done in the past." I explained to her that whatever she had done really was not the point—that she could be totally forgiven and cleansed and that her "who" was not dependent on her "do." I asked her if she was confident in her salvation and, when she quickly responded "yes," I told her that the Holy Spirit wanted her to be as established in believing she was righteous as she was established in her salvation. It is one thing to "know" a matter; it is another thing altogether to be established in it.

As I listened to this woman, I knew the struggle that was raging within her because I had fought the same battles. I *knew* she could win that war if she could understand in her heart the truth and power of Jesus' work on the Cross; and I knew that her life and her view of herself could change forever if she could grasp the revelation that she had already been made righteous and acceptable to God because of what Jesus did for her, for me, and for you on the Cross.

Righteousness Revealed

I remember the first time the Holy Spirit began to open my eyes and show me the truth of who I really was.

It was staggering, mind-blowing and almost too good to be true. I had been in prison for several months when I began to sense the Holy Spirit prompting me to begin to confess God's Word aloud. I will never forget the morning I was in my cell, and the Holy Spirit spoke to my heart and told me to confess 2 Corinthians 5:21: "For He made Him who knew no sin to be sin for us, that we might become the righteousness of God in Him." That was the first time I remember seeing this scripture, and its words were like a shaft of light hitting my heart, penetrating years and layers of darkness and lies.

It is one thing to "know" a matter; it is another thing altogether to be established in it.

In an instant, I could see that all my life I had thought something was wrong with me. I had always felt defective in some way and believed that I was rejected. I had always felt like a total loser. This scripture challenged everything I had ever believed about myself and began to reveal to me who I really was.

After the Holy Spirit showed me this amazing scripture, I took my Bible into the television room, a place that was usually empty and quiet in the mornings. Putting my flip-flops on the floor so I could kneel down on something other than cold, hard tiles, I opened my Bible again to 2 Corinthians 5:21. That moment is still as real to me today as it was then. I silently read the scripture one more time: "For He made Him who knew no sin to be sin for us, that we might become the righteousness of God in Him." Then I knew what I needed to do next—confess the Word aloud and believe it personally. So I said, "Lord, You became sin for me." (That was the easy part.) "Lord, You became sin for me so I could become the righteousness of God in Christ. I am the righteousness of God in Christ."

Hearing myself say aloud, "I am the righteousness of God in Christ" sounded like a lie because I had believed so differently all my life. But I knew the Word was true and superior to any of my thoughts or ideas—even the ones I had had about myself for many years. Because I was committed to believe and live by the truth of God's Word, I knew I needed to embrace the fact that God saw me differently than I had ever seen myself. So when I read that Jesus was made sin for me so I could be made righteous, the process of transformation had begun by the renewing of my mind.

> Because I was committed to believe and live by the truth of God's Word, I knew I needed to embrace the fact that God saw me differently than I had ever seen myself.

Finding Yourself in the Lord

Looking back, I realize that the journey toward understanding righteousness is a powerful process of discovery—one that has truly changed my life and will do the same for you. As I think about this, I am reminded of a scene that often took place in my childhood home.

When I was a little girl, I loved standing *really* close to my mother as she cooked in the kitchen. More often than not, I could be found right under her feet. On occasion, when I was impeding her progress as she prepared dinner, she would say, "Mary, go find yourself!"

I always responded, "But Mom, I'm not lost!"

Actually, I was lost for many years until I experienced finding myself as I discovered my true identity in Jesus. Before that, I had looked to everything the world had to offer—relationships, achievements, possessions, education, career, money, social pursuits and other activities—and still I could not find myself until I discovered how God saw me and realized that my true identity could only be found in Him.

I believe the Lord is saying to you today, "Go find yourself. Find who you really are in Me"; and I know that He wants to help you in this process. I pray that this booklet will draw you into the truth of the Word so you will discover who you really are.

> It is time to let the Word define us; it is time that we truly begin to see ourselves as the Lord sees us.

All of us can be tempted to look for our identity in every possible place in the world except the Word of God. It is time to let the Word define us; it is time that we truly begin to see ourselves as the Lord sees us. He has given us His Word so we will know the truth of who we are and be empowered to live as His chosen, victorious and glorious Bride, advancing His Kingdom as His able army in the midst of the dark days in which we live.

Yes, you have been chosen and accepted, and it is time to break the power of the lies you have believed, maybe all of your life, so you can overcome every obstacle that stands before you and live in victory and the truth that you are righteous. It is time to find yourself in Him.

Chapter Two

Journey Toward Identity

I didn't think my life could get much worse. There I was—everything that had once held me together and made me feel worthy had been taken away. I was in a federal women's prison with all the trimmings: black steel-toed boots, a thin pale green t-shirt, bulky white athletic socks and thick khaki prison pants made by inmates at another institution. There I was in my newly assigned clothing, sitting on a flimsy bunk in a lonely prison cell. As I slowly faced the reality of my dreary circumstances, I felt that I was in a prison inside of a prison.

Before I sank into total despair that day, I remembered that I had had an encounter with God several weeks earlier, when God sent a stranger to pray for me during visitation time. As a result, I had come to a firm belief that He would help me and be with me through my prison journey. *If God is really going to help me,* I thought, *I need Him right this minute!* So, alone in my cell, I closed my eyes to pray. Before I could even give words to the pain in my heart, I had a vision.

I saw the hands of the Lord, palms up, being extended toward me. As they moved closer, I could see that words were written on both of His palms. On the left hand were these words: *reject, felon, loser, thief, liar, failure, defective.* (I could immediately relate to these.) On His right hand, these words were written: *My beloved, chosen, righteous, anointed.* (These words were meaningless to me.)

Then His palms came a little closer together, as I heard the Lord firmly say, "You choose. You choose who you are. The world has called you 'a loser, a felon and a reject' but I call you 'My Beloved, anointed, chosen and righteous.' You choose. The words you agree with will determine how you see yourself; and the way you see yourself will guide your life in many ways. Mary, you choose."

This encounter with the Lord would forever change my life and teach me the important lesson of the power of choice and agreement. I did not realize how much destruction and pain had come from agreeing with the labels of the world, the devil's deceitful definitions and the pain of my past. Even finding my self-worth in my education and business successes had proven so faulty; I was in prison, and I certainly was not going to receive any accolades there. But the Lord was giving me a strategy for freedom. He was showing me a way out of the emotional prison I was in while I was also behind physical bars. This vision gave me the answer to one of my root problems—I didn't know who I was in Christ.

> The vision gave me the answer to one of my root problems—I didn't know who I was in Christ.

Step-by-Step to Freedom

The Holy Spirit began leading me on a wonderful journey of unweaving the tapestry I had assembled in my mind, producing a false image of who I thought I was. He showed me that years of believing the enemy's lies had formed a distorted self-image in me and caused my personality to develop certain traits I thought would never change. My negative self-image also influenced my choices, attitudes, and perceptions—things I thought would always be part of me. My life had been characterized by repeat performances, all of which were based on the lies I had believed and fueled by the thought that I could never change. I came to believe that the way I had turned out was just who I was.

Looking back, I see the intentional, devious plans of the devil to totally capture, torture and control me with these lies. But the Lord knew my bondage and began leading me on a step-by-step walk of freedom that would change me in ways I could not even imagine.

After seeing the vision of God's hands and understanding that my beliefs about myself did not line up with His Word, I began confessing the scriptures that expressed the Lord's perspective on my identity. (Some of these scriptures are available in the back of this book so you can confess them too.) The gap between my beliefs and God's truth was enormous. It was as if a torrent of rushing water had been flowing in one direction in my mind for years, forming a valley in the ground; but when I began to speak these verses aloud, the flow of water began to slow slightly. It took meditating on and confession of the scriptures aloud for a long time for the water to finally stop flowing in that direction and head down another path.

I did not completely understand the importance and the power of renewing my mind until I began following the Lord in this area. By renewing my mind according to His Word, I soon found myself being established in the identity that comes from the Lord. I was not merely gaining head knowledge; I was building a new foundation for my life and my future. Using the Word to destroy and replace the internal image I had created with thoughts and emotions that were contrary to God's truth was a vicious battle that demanded perseverance and determination, but it was absolutely worth the effort!

> By renewing my mind according to His Word, I soon found myself being established in the identity that comes from the Lord.

Victory Is Sure

All of us are in a fierce war with unseen forces that desperately want to keep us in bondage to lies that try to convince us that the truth about our righteousness in Christ is not for us on a personal level. Power is being released right now to ensnare you in the lies of the enemy and to convince you that you aren't worthy to be righteous, that you could never deserve to be righteous, and that you don't qualify to be righteous because of what you have done or neglected to do. But the power of God's Word is greater than the power of these lies. Remember that every demonic force is "overcome-able."

No matter what scheme the devil has unleashed to bring destruction and devastation against you and in your life, the Lord longs to reverse it and give you abundant life. For that to happen, you will need to come to a place of deep determination and be willing to keep pressing on with Him until victory comes.

I want to help you be prepared for the enemy's resistance as you attempt to break out of your past and walk in freedom. You must be determined to stick with it, to stay in the Word, confessing and praying the truth of who you are until you can look someone directly in the eye and say from your heart, "I am the righteousness of God in Christ." Once this revelation is established in your heart, you can get to such a place of stability that when you "do" something that does not reflect righteousness, you still know you "are" righteous. That is where you are going; that is the journey on which this truth will take you.

> No matter what scheme the devil has unleashed to bring destruction and devastation against you and in your life, the Lord longs to reverse it and give you abundant life.

The truth that righteousness is only found in Jesus will shatter the distorted self-image forged by years of rejection, shame, pain, performance, doubt and fear. It will put worldly power and success in their place in your life, break the power of living life to perform for others, and produce the inner peace and stability I believe you are longing for. So, be determined to endure and persevere until you know that you know that you know who you really are in Jesus!

Chapter Three

Your Destiny Depends on It

I believe that you have a deep desire to fulfill God's destiny for your life, and the revelation of righteousness is critical as you discover and pursue the purpose for which you were created. Perhaps you have never considered the correlation between righteousness and destiny, but I want you to know today that a revelation of your righteousness in Christ will help equip and empower you to be and do everything God has planned, chosen and ordained for you.

Be and Do

Notice that I write to you of "being and doing" everything God has planned as you fulfill your destiny. The order of these words is important, for we cannot achieve

God's highest and best purposes unless we first know who we are and then know what we are to do. Many times, we emphasize the outward actions we believe God has called us to take—whether they are acts of obedience, the exercise of a gift or embarking on a certain course of career or ministry—and neglect the most important aspect of destiny, our hearts.

You see, destiny is not just "doing;" it is doing out of being, and our doing will always be limited by our being. Just "doing destiny" is nothing more than religion. We can exercise our gifts, even as a way of trying to serve God, and still not fulfill our destinies. Destiny is more than a job, a ministry, or a great achievement; it a holistic pursuit that involves our motives, understanding, values and, above all, revelation of God's truth.

> ...destiny is not just "doing," it is doing out of being, and our doing will always be limited by our being.

A Life-Changing Revelation

A revelation of your righteousness in Christ will empower you to fulfill your destiny because it will enable you to:

• enjoy God's full and unconditional acceptance;

24

- have confidence in the fact that God has called and chosen you;
- experience increased intimacy with the Lord;
- gain strength for victory in every battle;
- be steadfast through life's storms;
- feel good about yourself;
- develop greater faith in the true nature of God; and
- relax in the knowledge that God loves you, no matter what.

The revelation of righteousness is so important and powerful that the enemy seems to fight it with a vengeance in every believer's life. One of the primary ways he tries to keep us from knowing who we are in Christ is through entrapping us in "sin consciousness." This term may be new to you, but if you are like many people, you could be living in its bondage without knowing exactly what to call it, how it affects you and how to get free from it.

Let me explain: Your consciousness is the inner awareness, the "internal influencer," that causes you to initiate and respond in certain ways. It directs how you feel about yourself, what you think, how you perceive people and situations and how you behave—and it operates either from a basis of sin or from a foundation of righteousness. Sin consciousness will make you fearful, hesitant and insecure about the pursuit and fulfillment of your destiny, while righteousness consciousness will give you the confidence to forge ahead without reservation into everything God has for you.

Righteousness must be defined on God's terms. We all have an innate need to be in right standing with God, but many are attempting to obtain this by terms they define. God says we are righteous because Jesus gave us His righteousness when He took our unrighteousness on the Cross.

> God says we are righteous because Jesus gave us His righteousness when He took our unrighteousness on the Cross.

We seek to be righteous by how much we accomplish, how well we perform or how we measure up to certain standards. This pursuit of man-made righteousness is bondage, and it does not produce the strength and power that result from knowing we are the righteousness of God in Christ, which comes only by faith. Living by preset, man-made standards only produces sin consciousness.

The Struggle of Sin Consciousness

I believe that living from sin consciousness is a root cause of so many of our problems and many types of bondage. It not only distorts our self-image, it also devastates our faith. If one or more of the phrases below describes you, there is a good chance you are living from sin consciousness and struggling to make progress in God's plan for your life:

- thinking endlessly about weaknesses and what you can't do;
- focusing on shortcomings—what you didn't do, what you should have done, what you could have done—not what you have done;
- having a constant sense of inferiority and unworthiness that dominates you;
- feeling guilty all the time and being unable to shake off condemnation;
- criticizing and/or judging yourself and others;
- feeling insecure and/or rejected;
- being easily threatened by other people's gifts and callings;
- wanting to hinder the spiritual development of people around you;
- being filled with fear, especially being afraid to step into your place of authority, influence or gifting;
- attempting to manipulate and control situations so your strengths are on display and weaknesses stay hidden;

- living in doubt, which hinders you from accepting the truth that you are righteous;
- identifying only with sermons or teachings on sin and not being able to accept compliments or words of encouragement;
- feeling like a failure;
- thinking God loves everyone except you;
- feeling that everything that goes wrong is somehow your fault; and
- trying to gain approval or acceptance through performance.

Furthermore, when you live from sin consciousness, you feel that you constantly "miss the mark," that you are never quite "good enough" for the Lord or other people or that you must "do better" in order for Him to really accept you. No matter what you do, you don't think you measure up.

If you are thinking, *I feel this way all the time!* you are not alone. In my ministry travels, I have encountered many people who are living far beneath their privilege as believers. But there is good news! These feelings of worthlessness and inferiority can be eliminated and replaced with a fresh sense of confidence and belonging by understanding the reality of righteousness.

The Rewards of Righteousness

As you grow in your understanding of your position of righteousness, you will not only have new strength and confidence toward God's destiny for your life, but you will also:

- focus on the abilities God has given you and how you can use them in His Kingdom;
- develop a "can-do" attitude;
- have a constant sense of being at peace with God;
- live with a strong sense of inner security;
- view other people's gifts and callings as part of God's team, not as a personal threat;
- look for ways to encourage others and help them move forward in their destinies;
- boldly take steps to progress in your call and destiny as divine opportunities arise;
- realize your worth and value to God;
- believe you will triumph in all things, being confident in God's help;
- stand firm in your position of righteousness in God and believe that the work of the Cross applies to you in the most personal way;
- receive God's forgiveness and move forward easily, with the ability to separate conviction from condemnation;

- be able to admit weaknesses and strengths with humility and honesty;
- gain proper perspective on situations and circumstances that involve you, without having a false sense of responsibility or guilt when something goes wrong;
- feel free to be yourself without feeling you must perform to be accepted;
- not be afraid to fail; and
- demonstrate grace toward others and toward yourself.

The kind of life described in the preceding phrases has already been provided for you. It is part of what Jesus purchased on the Cross, and it is available to you through faith. At the Cross, an amazing exchange took place for you. Jesus not only put to death the bondage of sin and the inability to have intimate communion with God; He also eradicated the unrighteousness that kept you from intimacy with Him. He not only provided salvation when He died and rose again; He also gave

> Jesus not only put to death the bondage of sin and the inability to have intimate communion with God; He also eradicated the unrighteousness that kept you from intimacy with Him.

you His righteousness, which makes you holy and acceptable before God, with free and unlimited access to His presence. Understanding the amazing exchange at the Cross is the beginning of the revelation of righteousness—a revelation that will totally transform your view of yourself, your concept of God and your ability to passionately pursue and fulfill His destiny for your life.

Chapter Four

It Started in the Garden

I am sure you realize by now that I believe one of the most vital, foundational revelations of our faith is knowing who we are in Jesus—getting our identity from Him and living our everyday lives with the sense that we are righteous because of what He did for us on the Cross. The Lord deeply desires for you to understand this on a personal level. When this truth is established in your heart, it will free you, heal you, fuel your faith and enable you to fulfill God's destiny for your life. The enemy knows how powerful this revelation is and will use many tactics to block and steal your understanding of it. One of his primary weapons is an attempt to trap you in sin consciousness.

After you are born again, you have the power to live

your life from a position of total righteousness because of your faith in Jesus' work on the Cross. The enemy wants to keep you blind to the truth of what happened there; he wants to deceive you by causing you to believe that you are simply "a sinner saved by grace." Although this phrase may sound holy, it is not true in the sense that you are not still a sinner after you have been saved. You may still sin, but the minute you accepted Jesus as your Lord and Savior, you became a new creation with a new nature—a nature that never existed before (see 2 Corinthians 5:17).

> After you are born again, you have the power to live your life from a position of total righteousness because of your faith in Jesus' work on the Cross.

You were changed from "sinner" to "saint" the minute you were born again. You were a child of the kingdom of darkness, but now you belong to the Kingdom of God. Your "who" (your spirit-being) has totally changed! Your "who" has been recreated in the image of God, and your spirit now has God's righteous nature. As you mature in the Lord, this new nature begins to affect your "do" (your patterns of thinking, your emotions, your choices and your actions). Your life once reflected the principles and values of the kingdom of darkness; you now begin to reflect the principles and values of the Kingdom of

God. Where did that righteous nature come from? At the Cross, Jesus took your unrighteousness and gave you His righteousness. At the Cross, an amazing exchange took place, one that restored you back to right standing with God and gave you a righteous position with Him. The revelation that your spirit-being has been absolutely and totally transformed when you were born again will enable you to keep a righteousness consciousness.

Shifting from Sin Consciousness

Let's take a look at why every person needs the righteousness found only at the Cross. In Genesis 1:26, 27, we see that God put Adam and Eve in the Garden of Eden to live there and take dominion over the whole earth. He gave them the freedom to eat of anything in the garden, except the fruit of one tree because eating that fruit would cause them to die. When Adam and Eve willfully disobeyed God, they shifted from having their consciousness based in righteousness to having a sin consciousness. This act of disobedience also brought sin consciousness into the heart of the whole human race.

We know that after Adam and Eve ate from the forbidden tree, they did not die physically, but they did die spiritually by shifting from having a righteousness conscious to a sin conscious. Their fallen state has been passed on to the generations throughout history.

When Adam and Eve intentionally sinned against God and committed treason, they forfeited their right to rule and have dominion and transferred their authority to the devil. This began the time when they had to live their lives separated from God because of sin.

Some of the immediate effects of this tragic event are seen in Genesis 3:7-12, when Adam and Eve tried to hide themselves from God, were afraid of Him and began to experience fear and shame. These were some of the first fruits (or results) of unrighteousness and marked the beginning of mankind's living from a sin consciousness.

God is in the process of restoring righteousness consciousness in the hearts of His people. To live with a righteousness consciousness, we must understand what happened at the new birth. Basically, before we accepted Jesus, we had the nature that was passed down from Adam and Eve after the fall in the garden. After we are born again, we become brand-new creations—creations who did not exist—and we received the nature of our Father in heaven (see 2 Peter 1:4). Simply put, before people are born again, they are in the family of the devil, and after being born again they are in the family of God and they are children of the King.

Now it is easy to understand why people who have not been born again act like the devil—because they are acting like their father. You might ask, "How can people who are born again and have God's nature act like the devil sometimes?" One reason is that they do not have the revelation of *who* they are and *whose* they are. Even after a person is born again, his or her mind needs to be renewed by the Word. Being born again is just the beginning. Our "who" is totally transformed at salvation, but our minds, wills, emotions and behaviors merely begin the process of renewal at that point.

It is so important to understand that our inner beings become totally different at the moment of salvation. After

> When Adam and Eve willfully disobeyed God and ate the forbidden fruit, they shifted from having their consciousness based in righteousness to having a sin consciousness that separated them from God.

being born again, we have only entered the Kingdom of God, and the awesome journey of discovering its riches is still unfolding for all of us. We have to allow our born-again experience to transform our souls in practical ways so the life of God in our spirit is expressed through what we think, say and do. That is why Paul says we need to "work out our salvation" by allowing the life of God that changed our inner beings to transform the rest of us: our minds, our wills, our emotions and our actions (see Philippians 2:12). We must seek revelation about our new identity in Christ and ask the Holy Spirit to open our eyes so that we may see ourselves as He sees us. We need His help to shift us from being sin conscious to being righteousness conscious. After being born again, you and I are no longer "sinners saved by grace"; we are the righteousness of God in Christ—and we sin occasionally. These two perspectives are extremely different and will produce extremely different results in our lives.

> After being born again, you and I are not "sinners saved by grace"; we are the righteousness of God in Christ—and we sin occasionally.

Solving the Sin Problem

When Adam and Eve fell, God knew that spiritually dead people could not fellowship with Him or be in His presence, but He had a plan to solve this traumatic problem that separated Him from the people He created and loved. He made provision for the sins of His people to be atoned for by the sacrifice of bulls and goats. In the

Old Testament, God instituted the sacrificial system, in which the High Priest entered into the Holy of Holies once per year to make atonement for spiritually dead Israel. The word *atonement* means "to cover"; it does not mean "to remove." So the blood of the animal sacrifices merely covered the sins of the people for one year; it did not remove their sins forever.

This gives us a picture of what was to come centuries later when God would initiate a New Covenant through Jesus, by the shedding of His blood on the Cross. God receives Jesus' blood as full payment for our sins and our sinful natures because His blood is spotless, pure and without sin—the only kind of blood that can satisfy the payment God requires for sin. Through the price paid at the Cross, God totally dealt a once-and-for-all lethal blow to sin consciousness and destroyed our sin nature. But each person must personally receive this gift of righteousness and believe in Jesus as Savior and Lord in order to experience the reality of the exchange of a sinful, fallen nature for the nature of God.

> The word *atonement* means "to cover"; it does not mean "to remove."

This is the essence of being born again. When you receive Jesus as your Lord and Savior, as the sacrifice for your sins, and acknowledge Him as Lord and the only way to be reconciled to God, you are radically trans-formed in the innermost part of your being. You are born again with a totally different nature—the nature of your heavenly Father.

Jesus Became Sin

By the divine plan of God, Jesus took your place. Jesus became sin. He did not simply take on your sin; but the Word says He *became* sin so that we could *become* righteous. Think about this: "For He made Him who knew no sin to be sin for us, that we might become the righteousness of God in Him" (2 Corinthians 5:21). This is part of the divine exchange that happened at the Cross. Jesus became what we were so we could become what He is. Jesus became sin for us, and we became righteous in Him.

> Through the price paid at the Cross, God totally dealt a once-and-for-all lethal blow to sin consciousness and destroyed our sin natures.

Until we allow this truth to renew our minds and really see ourselves as the Lord sees us, the devil will have free access to our lives. The enemy will rule us, but this does not have to be! We were created to take dominion over the devil. The minute we begin to believe personally the truth that we are righteous through Jesus, the enemy begins to lose power over our lives, and we begin to live as chosen, anointed children of God.

The revelation of righteousness will deepen our understanding that we are living in the Kingdom of God. We must overcome the lies the enemy has told us for years; we must arise and believe the Word—that we are the righteousness of God in Christ. We have to ascend to the truth that through Jesus we are partakers of His divine nature, because it is from this place that we will live as conquerors in our everyday lives, have His perspective and advance the Kingdom of God.

Chapter Five

Truth-Based Living

We need to be able to recognize whether or not we have made the shift from sin consciousness to righteousness consciousness. One way to do this is to examine the fruit of our lives and allow the Holy Spirit to reveal the attitudes, motives and conditions of our hearts. In chapter 1, I listed some of the "fruit" (the results) of sin consciousness and of righteousness consciousness. I encourage you to review those lists now and ask the Holy Spirit to show you areas in which you need to continue to cooperate with Him as you move toward living a more and more righteousness-conscious life.

Roots and Fruits

We need to deal with the root problems in our lives,

not with just the fruit. What do I mean? Think about it: If you cut off all the apples from an apple tree and do not destroy its root system, more apples will easily grow the next season. The apple tree will not even labor or exert a lot of energy to bear fruit. It will not stress, strain or hope to grow fruit. It simply grows fruit because its root system is designed to produce apples. However, if you chop down the tree and dig up the roots, nothing at all will grow, and you will not find an apple anywhere in sight! Likewise, we must make sure that the root systems of sin consciousness in our lives have been totally replaced by root systems of righteousness consciousness.

> ...we must make sure that the root systems of sin consciousness in our lives have been totally replaced by root systems of righteousness consciousness.

For example, if you struggle with rejection and have someone pray with you to help you overcome this challenge, you will only have temporary relief if your feelings of rejection are the fruit of living out of a sin consciousness. But when that root system of sin consciousness is gone and a root system of righteousness consciousness is established, feeding and nourishing you, you will have the power to believe the truth that you are in right standing with God, that He loves you unconditionally and that you are totally accepted in Christ.

Two Sources of Sin Consciousness

You may wonder how a person becomes sin conscious. I want to point out that there are two sources of sin consciousness—two different reasons a person may be living with this root system and from this foundation. One source is an unregenerate soul. A person may be sin conscious because he has never been born again. That person has a nature that comes totally from a sin consciousness because his spirit has not been regenerated. He can be living either a good life or exhibiting behavior that is obviously sinful. That is not the issue. The issue is that his spirit is unregenerate and his foundational consciousness is based in sin.

The second source of sin consciousness is spiritual immaturity. A person in this condition is born again and does have a regenerate spirit, but he has not grown spiritually; he is still a spiritual baby in the sense that he does not have a revelation of righteousness. People who fall into this category of Christians do not really know who they are in Christ or understand their rights and authority as believers. Even though they have the nature of

God living in their hearts, they do not seem to experience much practical victory in their lives, and they struggle excessively with daily pressures and circumstances. They live from a sin consciousness, which causes them to act and respond in ways that can even make them appear that they are not born again.

One other scenario that is common with believers who have not received the revelation of righteousness is that they may have lives that look very "together" and holy, but struggles of condemnation, rejection, performance unworthiness and other types of woundedness are hidden deeply in their inner lives so that they try to live an outward life of victory merely through willpower, not through the power of revelation.

This is one important reason we need increased revelation of our righteousness. We need to mature spiritually to the point that the people around us can see Jesus in our lives; we need to make a difference in our spheres of influence; and we need to have power to stand strong, live in peace and stay in faith as the storms of life come. We need to be living from the power that comes as revelation is established in our hearts not merely from our willpower. As we become rooted and grounded in the revelation that we are righteous, our inner lives and outward behavior will reflect more and more of the

Kingdom of God in practical and powerful ways.

One aspect of this reality that will be a powerful and important tool for reaching others in the coming days is that the revelation of righteousness will give you great peace. If you think about it, walking in peace around others who are in fear has great power. If you know that you are the righteousness of God, you can have amazing peace, even in very difficult circumstances. Walking in this kind of peace is a very practical way we express the Kingdom of God to those around us.

> If you know that you are the righteousness of God, you can have amazing peace, even in very difficult circumstances.

The Power of the Cross

If we will be honest with ourselves and with the Holy Spirit, He will help us determine whether we are living out of the truth that we are righteousness or out of sin consciousness. Are we living out of the power of revelation or out of the power of our wills? We need to see that Jesus did not simply save us from our sins at the Cross. No, the Cross is much more powerful than that. When we believe that Jesus died for us personally, we exchange our unrighteousness for His righteousness. This is one aspect of the amazing exchange that happened when

Jesus died on the Cross.

Many people attempt to obtain righteousness from something they have or from something they accomplish. But Isaiah 64:6 teaches us that "We are all like an unclean thing, and all our righteousnesses are like filthy rags." I must admit I was shocked when I first learned the meaning of the phrase "filthy rags." This verse is saying that any righteousness we try to possess in our own strength, from our own sources or from our own accomplishments is as dirty as a cloth used when a woman is menstruating. Without the righteousness found only in Jesus, our worth is no better than filthy rags. I know this is a graphic picture, but we need to understand that without what Jesus did on the Cross, we could never approach God; we would be eternally separated and without any hope whatsoever. As far apart as we are from God without Jesus, we must understand how near we are with Him and who we are because of His work on the Cross.

> Are we living out of the power of revelation or out of the power of our wills?

Total Restoration

Jesus has completely restored to us the righteousness Adam and Eve lost when they sinned. Think about it:

God has restored righteousness to you if you are a believer. You aren't rejected; you haven't been left out; you are welcome in the presence of Lord. You do not have to perform to obtain approval or acceptance from God; you do not have to meet some standard of behavior that you have determined to define holiness; you do not have to do anything, *but* you must believe.

Through Jesus, your ability to fellowship with Him is restored. God longs for fellowship with you and has provided a way for it—and the devil wants to keep you from fellowship at all costs and block you from personally believing this intimate communion is for you. He wants to keep you in bondage to a man-made standard of living, one that perpetuates the cycle of performance and rejection you may have been on for years. Because of the freedom that comes from believing you have been made righteous by the work of the Cross, it is no wonder the enemy tries so hard to deceive people in this area with so many lies.

From the beginning, God had a plan of redemption that would restore the unbroken fellowship He knew sin would destroy. God loved you so much that He allowed His only Son to die a horrible death, so His fellowship with you could be restored and you could resume a life of fulfilling the dominion mandate He gave to Adam and

Eve in the garden.

God wants you, and His precious Son suffered and died to convince you of His unconditional love. Don't be ensnared by the enemy who would whisper to you, "This is for everyone but you." If you believe in Jesus, this is in the package: You are loved and wanted by the Father. He looked all over the earth and could not find one of you. He wanted one of you, so He made you. He has made you to be righteous in Him. It is time to break out of the "I'm not part of that" bondage and resist that spirit of doubt, rejection and unbelief that has been haunting you for years.

> God has restored righteousness to you if you are a believer in Jesus.

I believe as we see this truth with fresh eyes, the foundation of our faith will deepen, and we will walk in humility and with great assurance—even in difficult days—knowing that we are truly God's children, redeemed, chosen and righteous. Our faith will function with greater power and consistency as we grow in the revelation that we are the righteousness of God in Christ.

Chapter Six

The Source of Transformation

After we are born again, we are constantly in the process of learning how to live out of our new nature. Most of us have lived for years in deceived thinking and worldly perceptions. We have allowed our emotions to rule our lives and guide our decisions, but Ephesians 4:22-24 gives us insight into how to live from our new nature in practical ways. These verses make clear that we must "put off, concerning your former conduct, the old man which grows corrupt according to the deceitful lusts, and be renewed in the spirit of your mind, and that you put on the new man which was created according to God, in righteousness and true holiness." Here, we are instructed to put off the old behavior from our old man (before we were born again) and to put on the behavior of our new man (our new nature after being born again).

How can we do this? True transformation only occurs as we renew our minds according to the Word of God. Transformation does not happen as a result of willpower; it is not accomplished by simply wanting it or through a program of behavior modification. Even if we really desire to change and decide to change, we cannot change ourselves; it takes the renewing of our minds on the truth and the power of the Holy Spirit to reveal to us that we are righteous and we can now live from our new natures. I cannot emphasize enough how important it is to spend time in the Word, allowing the Holy Spirit to use its truth to shift and change our thinking.

> True transformation only occurs as we renew our minds according to the Word of God.

Willpower Won't Work

I started walking in tremendous freedom when I realized I could not change myself. I liken the process of being transformed to the process of baking a cake. You can put all the ingredients in a bowl, mix them together and put them in the oven, but you cannot make the cake bake. The oven actually does the cooking. Similarly, we can give all the ingredients needed for transformation (honesty, prayer, desire, time in the Word, guarding our hearts, etc.) to the Lord, but it is He who brings the change. We can never take credit for any growth or maturity we experience in Him. Yes, we can do our parts to cooperate with Him, but He is the author and finisher of our faith (see Hebrews 12:2). There is a balance. He changes us, but we co-labor with Him. As we stay teachable and available to the Lord, He will transform us in amazing ways.

Many Christians are trying to live victorious lives using the force and power of their wills, but we must remember that the will is part of a person's soul, not part of a person's spirit. Any changes that are merely brought about by the flesh must be maintained by the flesh, and this will wear you out! Change that is a result of willpower is behavior modification, and that is not what I am talking about here. Many people seek to take on the process of transformation by just deciding to "do" things differently. True transformation starts in your core, in your innermost being, with your mind being renewed by the Word, and the effect of this renewing process changes your attitudes, thoughts, motives and

> We can never take credit for any growth or maturity we experience in Him.

actions. If change in your life comes from the power of your will, then the result is not true transformation.

We need to remember that we are three-part beings: we *are* spirits, we *have* souls and we *live* in bodies. Our spirits are the essence of who we are; our souls are comprised of our minds, wills and emotions; and our bodies are the physical vessels that house and carry around our spirits and souls.

As believers, we are created to live out of our spirits (our innermost beings). Learning to distinguish between what is spirit and soul is something we mature in as we spend time in the Word, in prayer and in communion with the Holy Spirit.

> If change in your life comes from the power of your will, then this is not true transformation.

The key to dividing our spirits and souls is the Word of God: "For the word of God is living and powerful, and sharper than any two-edged sword, piercing even to the division of soul and spirit, and of joints and marrow, and is a discerner of the thoughts and intents of the heart" (Hebrews 4:12). This is a powerful truth—one the devil does not want us to understand. As we mature and learn to discern what is coming from our souls and what is coming from our spirits, we will learn to be led by the

Spirit, not by our emotions or soulish thoughts and desires. This will also enable us to seek change through the renewing of our minds instead of through our will-power.

The key to transformation, maturing and moving forward with God is to allow the Word of God to align our inner lives with its truth. That is how we give the Word first place in our lives in practical ways. It starts with allowing the Word to work on us.

The Battle Continues

The devil has a strategy to do everything possible to prevent people from being born again, but the Lord is working to draw everyone into a born-again experience. We join with His work in the lives of those around us through prayer, walking in the fruit of the Spirit and witnessing through various means. Once people are born again, the battle does not end there. The enemy then begins to employ plans and schemes to prevent them from maturing spiritually. He wants believers to stay im-mature, carnal, powerless and unfruitful—and he does this by attempting to stunt our spiritual growth.

Let me say it this way: Every person is a spiritual being who can be described in one of the three ways

Paul writes about in 1 Corinthians 2:13-3:4. The first is a natural man, a person who is not born again and does not have a regenerated spirit.

The second is the carnal man, a person who has been born again, but lives as though his spirit is unregenerate. This is a believer who thinks and acts in childish ways and has not matured spiritually or has been wounded and not healed. Even though this person is born again, he may not have allowed the Word to renew his mind or transform his will, emotions and behavior; or, he may not have allowed the Holy Spirit to heal his wounds.

> We need to desire to progress and mature spiritually so our lives will increasingly reflect the truth of who we really are.

The third is the spiritual man, a person who has been born again, possesses spiritual maturity and has a nature that responds to the truth. This believer has experienced transformation in his inner life to the degree that it is obvious in his everyday living.

We need to desire to progress and mature spiritually so our lives will increasingly reflect the truth of who we really are. I believe the Lord is causing many people to be unsatisfied with the way things are in their inner lives, to draw them to desperately desire spiritual maturity and experience the Kingdom of God so those around them are drawn to the Lord.

God is calling us out of our childish ways, into the deeper things of the Spirit. Simply put, as we are transformed from the inside out and as we mature in the Spirit, allowing the Word to change our minds, wills and emotions (which affects our actions and behavior) and the Holy Spirit to heal our wounds, we express the power of the Cross in practical ways. We need to remember that one of the foundational truths that will mature us is the revelation of knowing that we are the righteousness of God because we are in Christ.

Chapter Seven

A Closer Look

Only the sinless blood of Jesus has the power to totally remove the sin nature we inherited from Adam. Hebrews 8:6 teaches us that Jesus became the Mediator of a better covenant, which is based on better promises. One of these promises is that sin consciousness has been removed by Jesus' blood—not merely covered, but totally taken away from us, making us brand-new creations. So, if we are living with sin consciousness, we are living under the Old Covenant. We are to be sensitive to the Holy Spirit when He convicts us of sin, so we can repent and turn away from whatever He convicts us of; but we are not to live our everyday lives with the consciousness that we are sinners. This is not part of our New Covenant. Remember, we are not sinners saved by grace; we are the righteousness of God, and we occasionally sin. By faith in what Jesus accomplished on the Cross, we can live knowing we have been freely given His righteousness.

I don't think we fully understand the loss and damage that occurred in Adam and Eve's relationship (and all who came after them) with God when they fell in the garden. Absolute separation and destruction resulted that day and has been passed down through the generations, even to you and me. The only hope for our restored relationship with God was that it be done on legal grounds.

We do not have to perform the rituals of any sacrificial system or live up to some preset standard to be in right standing with God anymore. The legal and only acceptable payment for our redemption and reconciliation was sinless, spotless, pure blood. That is why the absolute sinless life of Jesus is so important to us. As Jesus lived and walked this earth, He was daily paying a price for us. He was choosing to please the Father, walking in obedience, resisting temptations, fighting the devil and living from His spirit, not his flesh, so that when payment day at the Cross came, His blood would

> By faith in what Jesus accomplished on the Cross, we can live knowing we have been freely given His righteousness.

totally qualify as payment for you and me, fully canceling the debt we owed.

As I began to look more closely into the scriptures about righteousness, I found Romans 1:17 to be very insightful. It reads, "For in it the righteousness of God is revealed from faith to faith; as it is written, 'The just shall live by faith.'" This verse is saying that part of the good news of the gospel is that this is where we can find our righteousness. It is found in Jesus, not in our good works; not in our accomplishments; not in our expressions of kindness to others; not even in our abilities to withstand and resist sin and temptation. Our righteousness is found in our faith that Jesus became sin for us and gave us His righteousness in exchange.

> The truth is, you already please the Father; you have already become His child; you have His righteousness and you are totally restored to fellowship and relationship with Him through Jesus.

Only believe.

You must begin to live from this place of faith, for it is there you will find a safe refuge from the storms of life. The enemy will come and tempt you to get your worth and value from others; he will want to lure you into a life that is dependent on pleasing people; he will draw you into thinking you will never really live up to the mark or standard of righteousness, but you should keep trying. He will whisper to you that there is something wrong with you and you really do not belong. He will try to trick you into thinking that God will accept you if you do enough "right" things. The truth is, you already please the Father; you have already become His child; you have His righteousness and you are totally restored to fellowship and relationship with Him through Jesus.

No Payment Necessary

I encourage you to keep a short leash on sin—meaning, the moment you are convicted of a sin, repent. The moment you repent is the moment you are restored. But have you ever felt condemned long after you have repented? The devil loves to trick you into feeling bad and condemned even after you have asked for forgiveness. There is a huge difference between conviction from the Holy Spirit and condemnation from the devil. When the Lord convicts you, He will call your attention to a specific thought, word or action that is sinful. By contrast, the devil will impress you with a vague sense of wrong that covers you like a heavy

> The moment you repent is the moment you are restored.

blanket that makes you feel like a loser, sense that you have been rejected or believe that you are distant from God, without knowing specifically why or being able to see a way out. This is condemnation, a trap of the enemy, and you need to resist it aggressively.

The Bible is clear: When we repent, we are cleansed immediately. We have no ability to pay for our sins; only the blood of Jesus has that power. It is time we shake off the weight of condemnation that we so easily accept from the devil, from others and from ourselves. E.W. Kenyon put it this way: "We have become the Righteousness of God in Him, but we have been living as slaves when we ought to reign as kings. We yielded without a fight when we heard the Adversary roar about our unworthiness to stand in God's presence. Every time we confess our weakness, we repudiate the finished work of Christ and belittle our own position and standing in Christ."

Before I understood this truth, I tried to help "pay" for my sins. I remember while I was in prison, the Lord showed me that after I had prayed and asked Him to forgive me for something that was not godly, I would feel bad for whatever length of time I deemed appropriate for the sin. If I thought it was a light offense, then I might only feel bad for about an hour—and then I would let myself off the hook. If it seemed to be a heavier offense, then I would feel condemned for several days. In my attempt to pay for my own sin, I was totally denying the work of Jesus on the Cross!

Sin does break our fellowship with God, but we need to understand that our "do" and our "who" are separate. I am still the righteousness of God, even when I have sinned. God is not always pleased with my "do," but He is always pleased with my "who." As we are firmly established in this truth, when our hearts are totally convinced that the Lord is on our side, that He is for us and not against us, that He loves us and is never angry at us, we will have inner strength that will anchor us during the fiercest of storms. When others accuse you, you will stand. When people reject you, you will not be moved. When circumstances try you, you will overcome. Because through the storms and circumstances that will come, you are still the righteousness of God in Christ Jesus. This truth remains.

> Sin does break our fellowship with God, but we need to understand that our "do" and our "who" are separate.

Chapter Eight

Righteousness Revealed in Romans

If there is one book of the Bible that has helped me understand righteousness more than any other, it is the Book of Romans. In this chapter, I would like to share with you several of the verses that have deepened my revelation of righteousness and some brief comments I hope will enable you to also gain greater understanding and revelation of your righteousness in Christ.

1. Romans 3:21, 22

    But now the righteousness of God apart from the law is revealed, being witnessed by the Law and the Prophets, even the righteousness of God, through faith in Jesus Christ, to all and on all who believe.

Romans 3:21, 22 are powerful verses! They teach us that righteousness is available to us without our having to keep the law, and that through faith Jesus took our unrighteousness upon Himself and gave us His righteousness in the great exchange of the Cross.

In the Old Testament, God defined the terms that would put people in right relationship with Him. These terms were the elements of the sacrificial system. In the New Testament, because Jesus fulfilled the law, the terms that put people in right relationship with Him have been changed. Righteousness is now defined as faith in Jesus' work on the Cross. In order to be righteous before God, we no longer have to follow external rules. The New Testament expresses righteousness apart from the law and reveals that our righteousness comes not from anything we can do, but through what we believe.

2. Romans 3:25, 26

> *Whom God set forth as a propitiation by His blood, through faith, to demonstrate His righteousness, because in His forbearance God had passed over the sins that were previously committed, to demonstrate at the present time His righteousness, that He might be just and the justifier of the one who has faith in Jesus.*

God's righteousness was put on display when Jesus died on the Cross. At the Cross, God wanted to make righteousness available for all to see and appropriate personally. He has transferred the righteousness of Jesus to anyone who will believe. He has spoken loudly and clearly that righteousness is available. The question is, "Will we only believe?"

3. Romans 4:1-4

> *What then shall we say that Abraham our father has found according to the flesh? For if Abraham was justified by works, he has something to boast about, but not before God. For what does the Scripture say? "Abraham believed God, and it was accounted to him for righteousness." Now to him who works, the wages are not counted as grace but as debt.*

Many times we refer to Abraham as the "father of faith," but he is also the "father of righteousness" because he is the first one to whom the Scriptures refer as righteous through faith. God said Abraham was righteous because of what he believed. Abraham's faith gives us insight into the righteousness that is now readily available to every believer under the New Covenant.

4. Romans 4:5-8

> *But to him who does not work but believes*
> *on Him who justifies the ungodly, his faith*
> *is accounted for righteousness, just as David*
> *also describes the blessedness of the man to*
> *whom God imputes righteousness apart from*
> *works: "Blessed are those whose lawless deeds*
> *are forgiven, and whose sins are covered;*
> *blessed is the man to whom the LORD shall*
> *not impute sin."*

If only we could see what David saw! David must have had a glimpse of the grace that was to come, when God would impute righteousness that did not require adhering to the codes of the law. David speaks of the blessedness this would be to man, but we must understand that the devil is trying to steal those blessings from us by keeping us focused on trying to work for our righteousness. One aspect of the New Covenant is that it ushered in God's new requirement for righteousness, faith in the amazing exchange of the Cross. David had prophetic insight into the time in which we now live—a time when we would not have to keep laws, codes and rules to be in right standing with God.

5. Romans 5:17

> *For if by the one man's offense death reigned through the one, much more those who receive abundance of grace and of the gift of righteousness will reign in life through the One, Jesus Christ.*

What a staggering truth—the fact that what happened in the garden so many years ago has affected every person born since. Even more staggering is the truth that what Jesus did on the Cross provided a way for the very same unrighteousness that came to mankind to be *totally* replaced by the righteousness of God. God had a plan to restore everything destroyed in the garden, and He has restored our righteousness through the great exchange of the Cross. True life is found as we find our righteousness in Jesus, not through works or performance.

6. Romans 5:20, 21

> *Moreover the law entered that the offense might abound. But where sin abounded, grace abounded much more, so that as sin reigned in death, even so grace might reign through righteousness to eternal life through Jesus Christ our Lord.*

It is extremely difficult to access the grace of God without a revelation of righteousness. Our righteousness is found only in our faith in what Jesus did for us on the Cross. Unfortunately, many people, including believers, are struggling and living lives that are distant and separated from God's grace. There can be many reasons for this, but one that Romans 5:21 exposes is the failure to believe and receive the truth that Jesus gave us His righteousness so that grace could reign in our lives.

7. Romans 6:13, 14

> *And do not present your members as instruments of unrighteousness to sin, but present yourselves to God as being alive from the dead, and your members as instruments of righteousness to God. For sin shall not have dominion over you, for you are not under law but under grace.*

The truths found in Romans 6:13, 14 are amazing! God has called us not only to receive His righteousness by faith, but also to be instruments of His righteousness. He actually wants us to help others experience the life-giving reality that people can be in right relationship with God through faith in Jesus. As we embrace and believe that we have His righteousness, our lives will reflect what we believe, and others will be drawn to Him. We live in a time when people do not believe in the absolute truth of God's Word. People will not care if you tell them, "The Bible says..." No, you will need to live a life that reflects the truth and power of the Word in order to reach others with the liberating and empowering message of God's righteousness. As you have victory in your life, people will listen.

8. Romans 6:16-19

> *Do you not know that to whom you present yourselves slaves to obey, you are that one's slaves whom you obey, whether of sin leading to death, or of obedience leading to righteousness? But God be thanked that though you were slaves of sin, yet you obeyed from the heart that form of doctrine to which you were delivered. And having been set free from sin, you became slaves of righteousness. I speak in human terms because of the weakness of your flesh. For just as you presented your members as slaves of uncleanness, and of lawlessness leading to more lawlessness, so now present*

*your members as slaves of righteousness for
holiness.*

Either way, we are slaves. We are either slaves to sin
or slaves to righteousness. Being born again does not au-
tomatically make us slaves to righteousness. No. We must
believe by faith that we have become the righteousness
of God in Christ and yield to this truth with practical
expressions that are evident in our everyday lives. Paul
reminds us that we once were slaves to sin, but now we
have been delivered from sin and have become slaves of
righteousness. We can easily be tempted into falling into
the trap of living our lives measured by our works and
performance if we do not personally believe that we are
slaves to righteousness.

9. Romans 9:30-32

*What shall we say then? That Gentiles, who
did not pursue righteousness, have attained to
righteousness, even the righteousness of faith;
but Israel, pursuing the law of righteousness,
has not attained to the law of righteousness.
Why? Because they did not seek it by faith,
but as it were, by the works of the law. For
they stumbled at that stumbling stone.*

These verses make clear that those who pursue righteousness through the law will never attain it, but those who seek it through faith will experience the blessing of knowing they know they are right with God. Many are still stumbling today because they think they are not good enough to be righteous, that they do not do enough to be able to claim a righteous standing with God. The fact that they have already been made righteous seems too good to be true. The truth will destroy the lies the devil has been telling you if you will only believe.

10. Romans 10:2-4

> *For I bear them witness that they have a zeal for God, but not according to knowledge. For they being ignorant of God's righteousness, and seeking to establish their own righteousness, have not submitted to the righteousness of God. For Christ is the end of the law for righteousness to everyone who believes.*

There are many people who have a zeal for God and live their lives energetically serving Him, but they are doing these things to try to earn God's approval. They do not understand that Jesus has already purchased the approval and acceptance they are seeking from God.

These external activities are noble and good, but when they are motivated by a desire to be established in God's righteousness, they are faulty. The only right motivation for serving God is a heart of love that is responding to everything He has done for us, including providing righteousness for us at the Cross. We desperately need a revelation of the Cross so we can submit to God's righteousness and not try to achieve it on our own.

Confessing Your Righteousness

I want to share a few of the scriptures that have been instrumental in helping me to establish the truth of my identity in Jesus. I personalize the verses and confess them aloud. I hope you will read and meditate on these personalized confessions for yourself, and I believe they will bring transformation and strength to your life, just as they have to mine.

1. I am a chosen generation, a royal priesthood, a holy nation, His own special people, that I may proclaim the praises of Him who called me out of darkness into His marvelous light (adapted from 1 Peter 2:9).

2. Now He who establishes me in Christ and has

anointed me is God (adapted from 2 Corinthians 1:21).

3. Therefore, as the elect of God, holy and beloved, I will put on tender mercies, kindness, humility, meekness, longsuffering (adapted from Colossians 3:12).

4. I will praise You, for I am fearfully and wonderfully made (adapted from Psalm 139:14).

5. For He made Him who knew no sin to be sin for me, that I might become the righteousness of God in Him (adapted from 2 Corinthians 5:21).

6. I do not have my own righteousness, which is from the law, but righteousness which is through faith in Christ, the righteousness which is from God by faith (adapted from Philippians 3:9).

7. "Lord, Your eyes are on me because I am righteous, and Your ears are open to my prayers…" (adapted from 1 Peter 3:12).

I pray that this booklet has helped you and will continue to help you along your journey of discovering your true identity, and that you will live an overcoming life in practical, tangible ways. I know many people are longing for the next "move" of the Holy Spirit, but we also need to know that God has already moved tremendously in a way that affects our everyday lives. The move of God I am referring to is the fact that God has moved us out of unrighteousness into righteousness through the price Jesus paid on the Cross. I am praying that, as you personally believe and begin to live your everyday life from your position as the righteousness of God in Christ, you will experience more of the power of the Cross and more of His awesome love!

Therefore we conclude that a man is justified by faith apart from the deeds of the law.
Romans 3:28

For Further Study

1. *Battlefield of the Mind* by Joyce Meyer

2. *The Latent Power of the Soul* by Watchman Nee

3. *Two Kinds of Righteousness* by E.W. Kenyon

4. *The Blood of the Covenant* by Mary Forsythe

5. *Solving the Identity Crisis* (teaching on CD) by Mary Forsythe